Winner of the L. E. Phillabaum Poetry award for 2014

BROKEN CUP

poems

MARGARET GIBSON

LOUISIANA STATE UNIVERSITY PRESS   BATON ROUGE

Published by Louisiana State University Press
Copyright © 2014 by Margaret Gibson
All rights reserved
Manufactured in the United States of America
LSU Press Paperback Original
FIRST PRINTING

DESIGNER: *Mandy McDonald Scallan*
TYPEFACE: *Whitman*

Library of Congress Cataloging-in-Publication Data
Gibson, Margaret, 1944–
  Broken cup : poems / Margaret Gibson.
    pages cm
  Includes bibliographical references.
  ISBN 978-0-8071-5642-1 (paperback : alk. paper) — ISBN
978-0-8071-5643-8 (PDF) — ISBN 978-0-8071-5644-5 (ePub)
— ISBN 978-0-8071-5645-2 (Mobi)
  I. Title.
  PS3557.I1916A6 2015
  811'.54—dc23
  2013041465

This book is for David.

A few years ago, I met with a Hindu teacher who had given a talk on the Vedanta view of the Self in Alzheimer's. I sat down with a small, soft-spoken man who wore a wrap-around orange skirt and an orange tee shirt. I remember saying tentatively that many people identified the Self with the body or the mind, or with memory itself. Yogatmananda offered me green tea and dark chocolate, and he began talking about a cup from which one might drink tea or other beverages. Over time, the cup stains, it might chip, but one can still drink from it. Eventually it cracks, breaks, and no one can use it.

"The body is like that cup," he said, meaning the body-mind. "But whatever you have drunk from the cup over the years," he said, "that remains with you."

CONTENTS

I.

SENTENCES

An Assay

to David

I.

::

I have a friend who thinks it's terrible *there are no answers.*

He doesn't believe in God, because God would be an answer
  one could know, and we don't know.

::

I say he believes without knowing he believes. He scoffs at that,
  and I think to myself,

the root of *believe* is *to hold dear*—therefore, *to live with caring.*

I admit I'm stretching the root, but my friend lives as if he's taken
  Pascal's wager.

He paints, stroke by stroke. He wagers. He creates a world.

::

Theoretical physicists believe there are six flavors of quarks.
Their names are *up, down, strange, charm, bottom, and top.*

They believe this. They eat breakfast. They go for walks inside
  the landscape of an electron.

::

But you, my beloved, who forget that you forget, and who make beautiful
  sense of the world, would dismiss such cogitations.

You would focus on the sheer joy of one breath, this one breath.

II.

::

If I identify with what stays, I am one thing; if with what flows, another.

I am a river in disguise.

::

A river knows that *place* and *once* are not fathomed, plumbed, or tallied.

::

When I stand at the edge of Main Brook and watch the snowmelt sweeping
    around the prow of stone

upright in the cascading torrents, I am of one mind.

::

When I straighten up, having lifted and lightly balanced mossy stones to make
    a cairn, I am of one mind.

::

When I bow before the tree whose roots slide over a shoulder of granite
    jutting out of the earth,

whose roots hold the stone steady, flowing past it and embracing the stone,
    disappearing into the dark Source that makes all words one,

I am of no-mind.

::

Is it so terrible not to have answers?

III.

::

I grant you, it's terrible to lose one's mind as, burst of light by burst of light,
    the neurons misfire,

unable to reach across synapses, making run-on sentences, eroded
    fragments, tangles.

In the metaphor of eclipse, *the mind is shadowed.*
No ricochet of radiant protons graces its surface.

::

Where did you grow up? You ask me. My story, you knew it once. Yours,
    too. Now you read your memoir

more moved than when you wrote it. The story's fresh, immediate;
    your depth of feeling no longer held in check by intellect.

You read the sentences, your lifelines, amazed.

::

Is it in your DNA, perhaps? A coded sentence,

You will, like your mother before you, be asked to let go of all you hold dear.

::

Our friend picks up his paintbrush. You put down your pen. Think
    of Sisyphus,

condemned to accomplish nothing—

sentenced to toil uphill to that resting place when the stone crests
and settles, tilts and tumbles down.

What is his mind at that moment?

::

I keep wanting you to tell me what you remember, what you
    know and do not know

as the stone rolls, as the river flows, as the root sinks deeper,
    as is its way, out of sight.

::

Eclipsed, the moon goes dark, but the moon is still there, a deep presence
    held in place,

disguised as an eddy in the river. These metaphors I believe.

::

Up, down, strange, charm, bottom, and *top,* hums the chorus
    in the background

as Oedipus, that beautiful man, snow-haired at Colonus, says openly

All is well.

::

And you, who were memory's scribe, this is now what you say—

I have been lucky. I have been lucky all my life.

II.

HEAVEN

The leaves are turning, one by one carried away in the crisp wind.
In one letter he penned,
Coleridge turned away, calling love
a local anguish he meant to leave
behind him. *Away, away,*
says the blue and gold day, and no one hears it but the wind, whose law
it echoes. The dog has a red ball to chase.
You pick a flat, perfect stone for the wall you hope to live long enough
to rebuild. I prune
briars, pick burrs from the dog's fur.
I teach *Come* and *Sit. Sit here—*
a longer sit beneath the cedars. The grass is freshly cut,
sun low, all the energy
of a summer's day rushing into bulb and root.
The dog runs off, returns. The stones balance
steeply. Good work. Good dog. This is
heaven. Sit. Stay.

REMEMBERING

Now it takes both of us to find the word that will finish
the sentence. "It begins with a B," you say,
and I think, *Perhaps*, watching as my mind turns mirror

in which I see a small child, the back of her dress
unbuttoned to show the delicate blue line that is her spine.
The child looks at us, a fixed glance over her shoulder.

A formal face—no. Not *formal*. *Solemn*. No, *grave*.
She is older than her years, this girl. Thus, B . . . ungraspable B.
"Boethius," you say. ". . . Boethius?" "No, *Balthus*," we say

in one voice. Together we smile and touch hands lightly.
We've done it again. The world returns to its fullness.
Out the window a branch of white flowers

brightens beneath the sheltering, repetitive descant of a dove,
and for a moment I ignore
the unchanging pallor of that still child's face.

SOME QUESTIONS

::

When did you first notice? The doctor asks.

::

The doctor gives you three words to remember—
apple table penny

He shows me the clock you've drawn, the hour
and minute hands reversed.

Count back by seven from a hundred, he demands.

What does any of it matter? You counter. *Give me a real question.*

::

Sweet ruin, I'm of a mind to want
Origin—
                    the Causeless Cause, the Sourceless Source

whose presence may be sensed only in stillness and wonder.
Or, not.

::

If Mind is a *hidden hermitage,* a dark wood—
who can track
                    a disease that sieves the mind of its contents?

Who is present for that subtle, first tremor—
that *too much* or *too little* of who knows whatever it is allows

seepage or surfeit in the brain?

::
Tell me, when does
the tempest begin? When the first splash spatters the windshield?

Or when, unnoticed, sun-fire lifts a stipule of moisture off a stalk,

pulls it into the traceless—then slurs into cirrus and cumulous,
darkening counsel and mood,

giving rise to windy thoughts?

::
You're doing great, the doctor soothes.

Now, what were those three words I gave you?

Do you remember?

::
And here it is, the driving rain, a seine of pinpricks,
a roiling that lathers the pond—

and we're drenched in cause and effects, each of us
caught off guard, out in the open,
wet to the bone.

REVISING

This man who loves things, he's moving things
from here to there in the house,
but not randomly—no, no. He moves
things to their rightful places,
and he has a motive and a cue for action.
For example, two paintings, shifted from
separate rooms where they've hung for years,
now share a common wall in the library,
where the setting sun strikes their gold-leaf frames:
corn shocks in a field, a loaded hay wagon,
a farmer with his pitch fork, now hung below
an Anglican, formal, silk-knotted, and embroidered
rendering of an open coffin, the bare
body (absent perspective) about to spill
out of the box, but it doesn't, held in place
no doubt by the upright bishops.
Behold the man, they seem to say. *Behold
the corn god who died for our sins.*
"They're both about harvest," David insists.
"But can't we just let things be?" I cry.
Because too much is changing, too much
is forgotten, misplaced. Because
I want each thing to stay where I left it,
where I want it, where I know it, keeping vigil
over our rife impermanence. Because
these things will live longer than we will.
Because he will forget their names, and ours.
Because he will die, and I will. . . . "Just tell me
why you keep moving things," the words
hardly out of my mouth, and I get it.
The house is his poem, the poem is his life.
He's revising—as I will this poem,
hitching one sound to the next sound,
shifting this image nearer that one,

coupling. Just this moment in the dusty
cupboard, he has juxtaposed the flawless
Mesoamerican bowl and the Japanese
bird whose beak I banged off by accident;
his mother's teapot, restored, next to a bowl
he bought right off the potluck table,
because he wanted the image of the Fisher King
swinging his ankles, whistling
in the quiet of his heart—isn't it all about
the heart, about accident,
appetite, repair, and original paint?
About rupture and relishing, wounded
flesh, and the joy of returning home
moment by moment, trying to know
the place, and the two of us who live here,
seeing into our true nature as if for the first time?

FORGETTING

Hayscent fern in one windowpane, in another pane
rhododendron, red barn siding—

you're staring out the west window, as if what you
see out there

might wake the inner word you want, that fugitive,
unfaithful word

wed now to silence. As we wait, I try to imagine
your brain as a window

fitted with white squares of mist—then frost, then snow
thickening on one pane,

on another, and another. . . .

Slowly the ferns vanish, scent and root. And now
I blank out

the several panes that frame two oaks and a rope
hammock . . . a void

where once were form and fragrance, tall trees
and the faint

pattern of braided rope—an impression printed on
my firm thighs

and onto the smooth underskin of your arms, after
we'd slept there

barely an hour, suspended in sunlight.

WINTER

::
It snows. And snows. We shovel
narrow pathways, out.
The blue moon isn't blue.

Windrows of snow
against the door, windrows of snow
blur path lines—

your hair, too,
snow at the temples, where a blue vein throbs.

Madness, this wanting to curtail
drifts of thought
that overspill line after line.

We shovel narrow pathways, out.
The blue moon isn't blue.

Smell the cold air on my skin.

::
"Do you know your mind today,"
I asked, impatient,
                and you replied,

"It's talking to the wind."

::
A clanging of Canada geese
arrows through.

::
It may be like this in your mind . . .

Snow coming down
we stand on the snow-lace road—our remembered

footprints fading behind us in a motley of snow
and stone and lichen, speckled oak leaves, snow.

Stand still an hour and, see . . . ahead now
so still,
                so white, the imprint of a thought

never forms. . . .

There's rigor to forgetting—and no turning back.

::
Thaw—and a mighty

wind, then clearing—
our thew and

heave to haul the sodden
pine branch
blocking the road.

In the
nightly downpour of dream—
a hermit, a stand of birch wood,

gold light—and yet

we're not spared
the discipline of ruin.

::
(At the bridge,
under a rain of grapeshot
Tolstoy's young

Rostov turns from the wounded,
looks at the sky—

how blue, how calm, how deep. . . .

He could wish for
nothing else, he vows
were he *there*

beyond uncertainty.) And fear—

let's not forget that sinewy
loneliness.

::
Nothing as stark, after snow
as these
trees, black and white
shafts in last light—

a stillness that is respite
from tumult, resentment,
and the trap of
"hating my anger."

(Just so Prince Andrei
let *that lofty sky*
high up there, clouds
moving across the Infinite—
and the Infinite
un-nameable and still—

fall into him, he whose
mystical body
had been opened
by the shock of a sudden wound.

There is nothing but
quiet and peace,
he said. *Thank God!*)

::
Rain all week, and now in the pond
thick ice sinks free and floats

underwater, a pallid corpse
oddly green.

Where there had been deer tracks,
pocks, and cracks,

there's a puddle of rainwater—
within it, boundless sky.

::

Remember these words, I tell myself—
you wrote them!

Closer to death I want great faith and great doubt.

Now you must live them. Now you must live them.
And it won't do, asking *why* . . .

FAR-HEARTED

Hear it? I'm whining. A downward
pitch, steep and swift,
into underfoot impatience

and complaint. But what on earth
did you say
that would elicit this *far-heartedness*?

I don't know. I don't know.

Just now the heart's in love with
self-envy. Sure,
I remember when things were

better, easier—I liked myself, then.
You're not at fault, nor am I—
am I? Let me

let the dog I am chew on this stick
a while longer—
then I'll pitch it far down

the snowy hill, over the thaw.
I'll watch dog go
skidding for it, bring it

home, chew on it some more.
Dog *loves* it,
this ceremony of the stick.

Ah, but Love is not indifferent;
so this jot of love
marks a turning point.

Nor is it arrogant or rude.

ROSEMARY

Bud-pierce, sun-talon, blood-briar—spring
insists on re-naming itself.

Are you prepared for the day he won't know your name?
And I might have answered,

Lord of milk and suck, Lord of straddle-these-thighs, what is

my name
compared to the ten thousand unspoken, solemn or spangled

names of God? And I might have answered,

I've forgotten how to prepare, I've forgotten how to pray . . .

but I am learning now
to retrieve stray wordlings that shake loose from his sentences—

chalice and shovel, hold me, buried root—
and to say them as a rosary is said, or a mantram.

And perhaps I can also pray

with the cutting of rosemary I scissored from a clay pot
on a sill of the sun.

Smell this, I say—

stroking his shoulders and his neck with an arabesque
of its green fragrance.

Smell this. . . . Who cares what we call it?

TASKS

The task of a human being is to transform suffering to joy.
—Sufi teacher

And along the way, there's housework.
Forget the computer, the checkbook,
the inscrutable repair of whatever
overheats or squeaks or ices over.
Never mind the wooden lamp post, rotten,
fallen on its face like a corpse in the wet grass,
which needs to be cut. Your allotted
jobs are to dust, fold the laundry, tasks
in which you take such unsung pleasure
I'm abashed. I'm sorting cutlery; I'm Job
in a bathrobe, wondering where oh where
in the wrong drawer you put it. "We'll make
a good wife of you yet," I nearly joke.
But look at you: so happy, I bite my tongue.

ENACTMENT

A bit of climbing vine, copied in silver
and cleverly linked—that was the tie
that bound me, the cord about my wrist,
the shackle. I couldn't work the catch.
Nor explain to you how to do it,
although I tried. You went for pliers—
the wrong tool. All the while, my voice
a rising crescendo, my eyes wild,
complaint and imprecation,
and deep within me an image of the ghats,
the self-immolation of pious widows.
And I've been good. I don't deserve
this. Why, why, why? And you,
standing by, wanting to help, you could
only blame yourself: *incompetent.*
That's when I calmed down, and the bracelet
snapped open and fell into the sink,
into the abyss of yesterday's whisper
far back in the mind, barely audible: *trapped.*

LOSING IT

What little I know, I hold more dear,
now that I take the daily
reinvention of loss as my teacher.
I will never graduate from this college,
whose M.A. translates
"Master of Absence,"
with a subtext in the imperative:
Misplace Anything.
If there's anything I want
it's that more people I love
join the search party.
You were the one renowned
among friends for your luck
in retrieving from the wayside
the perfect bowl for the kitchen,
a hand-carved deer, a pencil-drawn
portrait of a young girl
whose brimming innocence
still makes me ache. Now
the daily litany of losses
goes like this: *Do you have
your wallet, keys, glasses, gloves,
giraffe?* Oh dear, I forgot
my giraffe—that's the preferred
response, but no: it's usually
the glasses, the gloves,
the wallet. The keys I've hidden.

And when I get frantic, when I've lost
my composure, my nerve,
my compassion, I have
only what little I know to save me.
Here's what I know: it's not absence
I fear but anonymity.

I remember taking a deep breath,
stopped in my tracks. I'd been
looking for an important document
I had myself misplaced—
high and low, no luck yet.
I was "beside myself,"
so there may have indeed been
my double running the search party.
"Stop," you said gently. "I'll go
get Margaret. She'll know where it is."
"But *I'm* Margaret," I gasped.
"No, no." You held out before me
a copy of one of my books,
pointing to the author's photograph.
"You know her," you said.
We looked into each other's eyes
a long time. The earth tilted on its axis,
and what we were looking for,
each other and ourselves,
took the tilt,
and we slid into each others' arms,
holding on for dear life, holding on.

WORKING WITH STONE

Making a wall stone by stone
as you used to relish
doing, or stacking stone on stone
in the woods to make a cairn
is like building a sentence
word by word. If that's so,
this poem is a word cairn,
and the wall that shambles about
the woodlot, losing stones
to frost heaves and tree roots,
is a sentence that won't parse,
however long I tinker with it.
Today I'm wondering
what I can say, having listened
hard, without understanding,
as you explained a "position"
when it's only clear
that the words you utter don't
fit the thought
you claim is clear when it's closeted
in your head, failing when you try it
on your tongue. Some poets
go after "something not sayable"—
how one might describe color
or the idea of God. You're after
simply how to translate
the vivid _____ that stutters across
your brain, right hemisphere to left.
Imagine the . . . *frustration*
is too easy. Try *sacrifice*,
an unwilling one at that.
"Too long a sacrifice can make
a stone of the heart"—
you used to quote Yeats

when anger sent you off into a silent
retreat. "Come back,"
I'd call across the wall. "Let's keep trying."
That was years ago; you don't remember.
"I like being *provisional*,"
you do remember saying,
back when your life lay ahead
unbounded, and you were young.
Being provisional, is that my aim now,
out for a walk in the woods
with the dog? *Come here*,
I call, *Come here now*, and he won't,
preoccupied with scents made rich by rain.
Nothing promises us *now and forever*,
only *now*. And just now,
letting the stubborn dog
and everything else in my life
just be what it is—surely a form of
surrender—I muse
and shift from one outcropping of stone
to the next flank of ledge
half-buried in beech leaves,
lifting loose, irregular chunks of smaller stone,
their moss a green-fuse green,
still others unevenly spangled
by pastel ovals of lichen—
stacking the stones.
Raising cairn after cairn,
mute stone after mute stone.
Knowing that each cairn, or any
one stone, may list in place
or tumble, unbalanced
by the least leaf or spit of rain

before I return
to the stones, to lift and coax them,
to turn them—so much is guesswork—and try again.

CHANTPLEUR

This morning the little new
is a word I speak haltingly:
chantpleur. Quick now,
before it's lost in the swell of wind
as the pines around our house
billow, and rain drills the roof—
say it, *chantpleur.* Again,
chantpleur. Hear it; let it course
down your face. *Chantpleur,*
a compound noun that yokes song
with the act of weeping. A noun
is a verb that holds still,
that settles in one place too long
and casts a spell of apparent
permanence. We think we're nouns.
But really all I have to offer
is *chantpleur,* a word as impermanent
as the touch of rain on my skin.
A word minted by one who has heard
the wordless song of the wind;
by one who sings and hears
within herself a blended sound,
a diphthong for the lyric river
pulsing in her wrist, a river wrested
from what no one wants to hear:
We're losing him, he's fading away, he's not
himself, he's slipped through
a rip in the mist. He's with us, and not.
With us, and not. *Chantpleur.* Just look,
he moves his hands like birds as he speaks.
Every blessed word a winged
migration—flowing, flown. *Chantpleur.*

III.

RESPECT

::

Naturally rough-hewn, a scrawled uplift
of splayed shade, broken branches big as
ship's timbers—this wolf-tree sentinel,
just behind the tumble-down west stone wall,
this mix of living and dying, both at once,
it's my angel of history. Doesn't
respect mean *look-again*? "Pay attention,"
you used to caution your children, your students,
and me. So is that why, mute this morning,
you stare out the window at the wolf tree,
down at your hands, now outside at the tree
as sun and shadow mottle stone and wood?
"I don't understand why I'm like this,"
you say. Your hair is silver-gray, but I take
your hand like a child's, and we sit down
on the yellow sofa and settle the cushions.
You trace the splay of small bones on the back
of my hand as I talk about the forgetting,
how invisible it is. Had you
a broken leg, or a brace, "You'd know," I say.
"You'd see it plain." What tangles and knots,
what misfires and seeps away, who sees
that? Who sees that, I repeat, and slowly
something shifts, a dead weight
falls away. Respite, I think, as the light
returns to your eyes from somewhere inner.
You're clear—the way you used to be. Clear.

::

He wrote, *We're these wild-eyed centers
of perception.* He wrote, *We're a phylum
of night thoughts and summer fantasies.* He wrote,
I learn to listen to silence until it fills with snow.

37

And if he walked alone steep hills and ridges,
happy, in the solace of roots like the tendons
of a human foot, learning the patience of small
animals, staying out of sight, lingering in the
shadows, that doesn't mean he approved of
the withdrawal suggested by these lines.
He wanted to rid himself of idealism,
learn humility, join in—even if freedom
and justice might bring to others *the trouble*
we call help. I read his scrawled notes in the
margins of his poems to see how he argued
with himself, how nothing was easy. He wrote,

> *In a future dynasty of wealth and injustice,*
> *when the Chinese again become poets,*
> *they will read of our lives in time capsules*
> *and speak of the rich professionals of America*
> *with Oriental inscrutability and awe.*
> *How, they will wonder, did so many men*
> *of uncommon circumstance slide so easily*
> *into the ancient trap of spiritual depravity.*
> *They will wonder that a land of such surfeit*
> *had no curiosity, knew nothing of history. . . .*

When he wrote, *Inevitably, I'm Chinese,*
did he mean he was ready to write inside
the walls of a lean-to, a full moon flooding
the window? He'd just built his own house
in the woods and was *living in snow,*
believing in brush strokes—
once again embracing a life of outskirts
and simplicity, living with a great respect
for mystery and the pleasures of getting lost.
Now when he hears Odetta on the Bose sing

"Sometimes I feel like a motherless child,
sometimes I feel . . ." it's himself, a choirboy
in Bradford, that spiritual his solo,
that solo his lament for his mother,
who suffered and whom he couldn't help.
In my favorite poem of his, he's in a dream
at a banquet, and he rises, rises and anchors
on a chandelier, *looking down at faces*
for a reason why. From his perch he reads
a broadside as the waiters below him pass
and serve, rocking like ships or shadows.
He begins in the middle, saying,
Listen,

> *whenever you must die or choose*
> *to fight someone else's war, never*
> *wear an initial or a pin, a uniform.*
> *Learn to fly instead,*
> *shape your mouth like wind*
> *and push your breath to call*
> *whoop whoop*
> *whoop whoop*

and in the poem these words crack and hatch into
birds that fly above everyone's head,
floating in slow motion, floating out to sea.

> *I had dreamed of freedom.*
> *The waiters disappeared.*
> *The servants vanished.*

And so he sounded his barbaric *whoop*—
he was my Whitman, my Thoreau, my Li Po
and Po Chu I. He loved William Blake—

who pointed to children at play, whooping
with laughter, and said one word, *Heaven*.
He loved what hands and heart could make
together. Driving home, he'd shift gears
with his knee, his right arm around me,
he wouldn't let go. He tied trout flies,
sought the right curve of blueberry branch
to carve into a bird, gardened, taught
whoever would listen. In each of his
gestures or broken sentences now, I sense
memories that nest in the heart, more than
shadow-play. They're real, if inaccessible.
Taking words from his poems, weaving them
inside my own, what is this if not
another way of making love? He's given us
a body of work in which to find him.
I go there, it's another world, and I listen.
He said, *I like to think of things far off.*
I like to speak of good and evil. He said,
I refuse to count my losses. He said,
right here, right now: *Earth steams, birds fly north.*

IV.

HAPPINESS

An art, not a right, happiness,
according to the Dalai Lama
(David reads aloud to me),
is not as *elused*
as one might think, but *clozer*
and *grisp*. I wonder
if his screwing up
how words are said
is prologue
to a deeper detour in the neuronal relays . . .
or is it faulty eyesight
as he speeds over the lines
of small print?
Now he looks out the window
at a steady drizzle.
He smiles and calls it
"the seep and slur of rain."
He enjoys
punching out the stressed
syllables as he returns
to reading—
*a **measure** of **personal**
happiness*—happiness
our purpose in life,
not selfish as one might suppose,
although the wish to avoid
unhappiness
may be. And I remember
a friend's sad report:
"He put his urine-soaked
underpants on my face
one night as I slept."
She told me this serenely,
as if the experience

she had with her husband's
dementia would be mine, there
was no stopping it. I said nothing,
only fixed my mind
on the remembered smell
of David's skin—something like
saffron married to a whiff of ripe
pears and worn-out
cotton undershirts. Blindfolded,
I could distinguish David
and find him in a crowd of men,
were I allowed to snuffle
each man's neck and smell
the difference—
and that thought gave me
happiness
as unexpected as was the glimpse of the road
that moved beneath us
as we sped home on a morning
long ago, after
a night of reading each other's
poems aloud, every
blessed one of them,
the road beneath us seen through the rotting-out
porous floor
of the old jeep,
we traveled at the
speed of light,
and nothing, nothing
could slow us down
or keep us
separate from each other
or the road, wherever it took us.

WHAT IS IT?

Our friend looks at me across the room, shifts in his chair.

"I think of you—both of you," he says. "Nobody
these days does anything
that deprives oneself, that costs . . ."

He shifts again, looks away, clears his throat.

"It brings to mind the marriage vows," he murmurs.
"In sickness and in health?" I ask. "Until death do us . . ."
". . . *part*," he concludes. "Exactly."

Point blank now, "What's to keep you from leaving?"

"Nothing."

It's what he's feared and wants to hear.
"*Nothing.*" He repeats the word. He's won. He nods.

"But," I add, "I'd never do that."

And the word we haven't said aloud says itself in the silent room.

"Love's so fragile," he comments, his voice low.

"Yes. Also strong." Yet wondering
what is this *Nothing*
that holds me, that holds us, holds us all—*What is it?*

SPIRITS

He's sure they're here. Not the ones who misplace his glasses.
Not the wine I take at dinner—although a host of spirits
gathers with us at the table.

                  And not the ones holding hands
as they listen, evenings, to the Late Quartets.

He feels another presence, or more than one, in the room.

"Are they spending the night?" he inquires.
    "Who do you mean, the children? They're with their families."
He thinks they should be with us. "Did they borrow the car?"
    "There's no one here but us."

A raw cry in the woods, a rustle in the neural pathways—
he startles.
            "It's an owl," I tell him. "A *bard* owl,
another kindred spirit."

He nods, he knows I'm teasing his uncertainty—not kind,
I think, if to tease
adds fear to fear, fire to fire, fervor to fervor, and doesn't solace.

"I don't care about the owl," he whispers and kisses my neck.
"I just want to know you're here."

HOUSE ARREST

There is the fact of no-selfness, but here I am
smelling of flour and butter, my mind a raga
in an evening sunset of self-pity,
as Krishna Das is chanting, courtesy of a CD
on the Bose. There's a blur of tears
in my eyes because we are not—no, we are
finally not—going to India.
Even if we have tickets. Even if dear friends
are going with us, one of them
named for Gautama, the Buddha.
Therefore, *India*, the idea of India,
is like my *self*, at the moment
a distant perfume, or a false belief
in something imagined to be there.
My India is too much thought about,
not enough seen for what it is.
And that *what it is*, that impermanence,
I'll not see—because travel
is too hard, I'm too tired, and David has
forgotten how to remember
and might be overwhelmed by the traffic
and the noise of lives lived in the streets,
by unfamiliar beds and bathrooms.
Our other friends, and our family,
are relieved. But here I am
rolling out piecrust, and this circular
disk, meant to hold things together,
is not a mandala, is not a rudraksha,
nor a kapalamala, not a begging bowl,
drum, or bell. It is piecrust,
ordinary piecrust in the making.
I draw three lines in flour across my forehead.
Might as well be a Shaivite. Might
as well be the dancing god's raised

foot of liberation, not the dwarf
that's pinned beneath him. And if India
is burning to ash in the palms of my hands,
my feet are, despite everything, moved
to dance creation back, right now,
right here by the kitchen butcher block
floury with piecrust. I am
Shiva Nataraja, creation and cremation
in one visual theology—*do you see?*
Make do, whispers the Unmanifest,
as I try to relish last summer's
blueberries, fresh from the freezer,
hard as marbles and dark
as winter solstice
in the lucky dark of Connecticut—
India, a pedestal for my feet
as they dance down
ignorance, illusion, and the selfish wish
for pleasure.

You do not even have to leave
your room, Kafka said.

LIKE ICE

What is it about some people?

As I'm leaving his house after a convivial visit, my host, an old friend,
     stares at his shoes

and mutters, "I can't see much good ahead."

Is he Cassandra? Or yesterday's news? Does he mean to be saying
     he'll help out? Or opt out?

"There's always good," I reply, meaning *the sooner the better*—
     however one defines

or would embody the Sublime, it would be better if it arrived pronto.

Before David, intent on a mission he's forgotten, wanders off into the woods.

Before he shivers to see daylight wane and an undefined darkness slur
     along the window glass.

Before *I'm so glad* means *I just do as I'm told.*

"You think you have it bad," another friend quipped, too quickly, then
     pulled herself up short—

"and you do." I don't recall what she said next. With practice, one can

simply watch as an agony, like ice in warm liquid, dissolves without
     altering the level in the glass.

SUMMER

Inside *summer*
there's an Anglo Saxon at the mind forge
hammering out a trochee
for tree crickets and heat.
Inside *summer*
I lie down in the grass and listen
as wind swells,
a chorus of summer
words rising to the tip of my tongue—
honeysuckle, crabgrass, daylily,
plum. Inside *summer*
there's honey and evanescence
in equal measure, a ripe
clatter of syllables, then a space
culled and quiet.
Inside *summer,* summer lulls me—
then I remember,
and the spell breaks.
I sit up and stare at the chestnut tree
arched over
our border garden of phlox and summer lilies.
Unfair *summer,* unjust—
to be so full,
to be garner and gather—while you,
my beloved, grow daily more quiet, your mind
a summer sky
seen by one floating face-up in the pond,
sky so distantly brilliant

one holds one's breath, startled—chilled.

AFTER

I slip away into end of summer
light, to be in the company of trees.
Now, when the tall chestnut
rustles in the wind, listen . . .
it's like living by a river.
Is *river* a metaphor for the body?
Or for the soul? Is the question, *"What lasts?"*
or *"What goes?"* This morning, sky
is blue as the cord of vein on your wrist,
blue also a pair of dragonflies
in their mating flight over the pond.
I think these words are blue. They bow
their heads shyly, like James Wright's
ponies at dusk. Remember his poem?
At the end he steps out of his body.
And look, the boughs of the white pines
on the other side, they stir
as if floating in place, as if bowing
like swans, as if a spirit's been released,
and they honor it. Breathing in.
Breathing out. Left behind.
My great happiness in their loneliness
surprises me—we've just made love.
I'm sixty-six, more hesitant. You're
seventy-two, in your mind sixteen, our bed
a field of tousled Queen Anne's lace.

HARD OF HEARING

Curled in your lap, Clara
purrs—engine
and *primum mobile,*
a cue for contentment
in the confines of the moment.

And because there's more
than one way
to heaven . . . and perhaps
because Alzheimer's
has a purr in it,
mesmerized, I murmur
more to the fire
than to myself,
"Maybe we're entering
Nirvana. . . ."

Puzzled, you look over
and reply,
              "Entering *lasagna?*"

FINDING IT

Give me a moment
to remember, then to find in the ashes of my former life,

sweet solitude:

a fire that swirls and billows on the hearthstone,
a fire that resembles the reflection of light off water;

and fire-breath, that long exhalation into the moment,
this moment,

before the forecast snow arrives, before any hint of being stranded
takes hold in the mind,
                        so that the mind flows, alert and calm,

and body could simply lie down with the mind, in front of the fire
and make love,

no sign of forethought or urgency,
mind and body turned toward the fire, absorbed—

you may think, dear reader,

that this poem, which began to stir beneath a mask of regret
for the luxury of solitude lost,

now shows its true face;
that I'm marooned in desire, burning—and, burning, attached

to pleasure, therefore also to pain, to the sweet sting in particular
of holding on to what only slips away.

And yet this feels more restful than I remember desire to be.
Body and mind I am turned toward fire

just as a mother might
succor and protect her own child, body and mind

turned toward interior plenitude—
however brief, the source of solitude's wanting nothing else,

not even these words.

BROKEN CUP

I've forgotten how it broke, the great cause
or the petty cause that cracked the handle
into two pieces and left me without
a cup for morning coffee. In the cabinet
there were others of white porcelain,
with steeply elegant lines, cups that matched
their saucers. But my cup was Mexican,
squat, and as round as Rivera's peasant
bent before the wall of callas
he carried on his back, his burden of blossoms.
Hand-painted, my cup was carnival
purple and yellow, flowers that honored earth,
birth, death, geometry, symmetry, riot,
good sex, good coffee, the sun rising hot.
I banished it, broken, to my desk and used it
for paperclips. Now I've rescued it, fit
and glued the pieces back together.
Still I'm afraid to lift it, even to wash it by hand
in hot water—it is that fragile.

You brought the cup to me from Puerta Vallarta,
that seaside trip you took to help
your daughter past heartbreak—a little hotel
by the sea, with bougainvillea
and a great deal on cocktails as the sun
rolled its dying splendor onto the Pacific.
I think I was jealous; I was jealous. I hoped
you drank margaritas and missed me—
most likely Dos Equis with a squirt of lime.
The cup gave me Mexico each morning,
on the cheap. I loved it. *I loved it,*
it broke. I ignored it, I cast it aside—
sounds like a classic sitcom-bad marriage.
Sounds like the wary caregiver who reads

The Thirty-Six Hour Day, heart empty.
Who really wants to know about this despair?
I have minimizing friends who tell me,
It's not so bad—just a little accelerated
forgetting, such as we all have these days.
O Ancient of Days, that was once a name
for God, for something so deep within the self
it's beyond us. Even so, it is possible,
I want to tell them, to love what is broken.
Possible, urgent, and necessary.
And so for love of thee and me,
I take my broken cup and set it down
before me on a yellow place mat. I make
toast with ginger jam and real butter,
coffee whose beans have flourished
on a mountain in Peru, I hope near Machu Picchu.
I sit down in my Japanese bathrobe,
in my Navajo beads, with bare feet; I sit
without ire or envy, without fear or despair,
and drink and eat. Slowly. Very slowly,
savoring all I can remember of that first
night we met, the good talk, the dancing
until we were too tired to do anything else
but take the dancing to bed—the miracle
of unintended meeting, the first of what
was to be years of meeting, moments
I hope to remember when I lie down to die,
my beautiful love, your head of unruly hair
and unruly thoughts unraveling
into a silence that will lengthen . . . or may
break off, as this handle did, in two pieces.
Who knows how love will hold, or if we will
ever be all right. Who knows what *wrong*

tastes like or how much emptiness the cup
will hold as we share it—who knows?

And if it is the cup of suffering,
drink it down—or better, may it pass from you,
and you live easy and go gently
where you will, or where you must. I'll go
with you, grateful for plum-colored flowers
so close to bruising, coffee, sunlight, earth;
the journeys we took together—and the long one
left us to walk until we lie down near
clear water, shade trees, green pasture.
In that place, there will be nothing unspoken,
nothing forgotten or feared. Day or night,
whatever the hour, it will be all shining,
our whole and broken bodies full of light.

BED

::
"Well, we're not sixteen anymore," I say softly.

::
"Funny you should say that . . ."
and you begin
talking memory, as if we were
in fact sixteen,
mistaking me for some distant
virginal mist
rising off female skin
like fog off a lake.

"I didn't know you then,"
I reply. "I'm your wife
now—remember?
Happy also to be
your mistress, if you'd like."

We're laughing now,
under the covers,
your face near
my thighs. You come up
for air, a conspirator:

"Margaret likes that, too."

::
Making love takes longer,
We make reservations
as if for dinner out.
Afternoons for delight—
bed? Or sofa?
Well, isn't the body

a space-time event?
Isn't it a river,
or the color of the ridge
seen through winter woods
at four, when sun
spills gold on it, then
russet and purple,
dun and dusk?

::

"Your skin," you murmur,
"soft—here, feel . . .
so beautiful. It's so beautiful.
Here and now, snow
falling outside, and we're
warm, inside each other. . . .
                    Have we ever done this before?"

PAJAMA POETRY

As we're dressing for bed, undressing
from the day, I show you the label in back
and the fly in the front of your gray flannel
pajamas—but you're cold, you don't
understand. I explain *why,*
helping you remove your sweater,
but you're all about living
without the *why*—and the goose down
comforter I promised you means as little
to you as the future tense, or the past.
You're cold, and I'm tired enough to give up
and just *be* a down comforter—that's what I do.
Down I lie in feathers, mute. And so bored.
Or I write what Isherwood calls "pig poetry,"
a wallow in old pleasures remembered—
another way of saying, *stuck.*
You're stuck with the mystery of pajamas.
I'm stuck with the ritual of explaining
the mystery of pajamas. In this script,
I'm the prompter, or the cue card—glad for
the occasional grace of finding it
funny when you put on your shoes
in the middle of the night and come back
into our bed with them on. What good
would it do to ask "*Why?*" Or to recall
the years we slept simply in our skin?
If you stay with it, you can go with it,
and if you go with it, you can take it,
I remember your saying, happily,
out of nowhere, listening to Beethoven
at breakfast, *adagio cantibile,*
so that now lying awake in the dark
I hear your words as a little phrase
the flutes propose and pass on to the strings,

a melody that swells serenely,
breaks down phrase by phrase, ebbs, resurges,
repeats, then gradually resolves,
engaging the whole orchestra. No one
calls Beethoven's music "pig poetry."
Even what's stuck, "said" over and over,
is moving, inverting, changing key,
only to re-emerge from the ashes
as a firebird-crazy wisdom. We'll call it
"Mystery in A Major," or "A Romance
for Pajamas and Strings," a prayer:
May I stay with it, may I go with it
moment by moment, and take it to heart. . . .
Without asking what the *It* is, or why.

SOLITUDES

::
For today, I will memorize
the two trees now in end-of-summer light

and the drifts of wood asters as the yard slopes away toward
the black pond, blue

dragonflies
in the clouds that shine and float there, as if risen

from the bottom, unbidden. Now, just over the fern—
quick—a glimpse of it,

the plume, a fox-tail's copper, as the dog runs in ovals and eights,
chasing scent.

The yard is a waiting room. I have my chair. You, yours.

The hawk has its branch in the pine.

White petals ripple in the quiet light.

::
In the quiet, a necklace of gourds on the garden fence.

A mourning cloak on a seeded spray of crabgrass.

An undulant whine of cicadas.

::
We are waiting as, over a measure of time, the bougainvillea
in the pot by the door
puts out flowers—tangerine, then pink,

then a brownish-gray translucence
as paper thin
as the texture of the skin along my wrist bone.

::

I draw you a map, *out of scale,* to the fish store you want us to go to.

You make the pun to shield yourself from not knowing
where it is.

"I haven't been there for years," you insist.

And a map to a friend's house not five miles away.

"I've only been there once in my life." You pause. Then,

"That's what I remember."

::

What you remember becomes your truth; what I remember, mine.

I respect more clearly now
that blessed word
ours. And the curve of intimacy in the phrase,

two solitudes that border and protect each other.

::
"I used to remember who I am," you say in a low voice,
bemused,

as down the long hypotenuse from sky to earth,
a great blue

glides over the cedars, the green lawn, the white asters.
The dog doesn't sense it.

The heron becomes a stick in the reeds,
a broken angle

with an eye still intact—it looks through its own reflection
face to face;

then, when it lifts and flies off, after the ripples settle,
it's gone, you say—

no trace.

SIMPLE

God's joy, wrote Rumi,
moves from unmarked box to unmarked box.
I remember my sister's husband,
after her stroke, complaining
"Liz is a box. It says
on the outside *Liz,* but she's not there,
not the Liz I married." "Is she simple,"
our daughter wondered,
noting how the sheer
weight of loss
had rendered my sister speechless.
But I have to confess, as I watch
your memory fade—
grief and the rest of it aside—
I'm also curious: What is the self?
What of the self, or the no-self,
outstays loss after loss?
I watch the wind
fill with leaves, red and gold,
as the tree that was once
a summery billow
thins to an outline. A friend
told of a woman he knew
with dementia. "And who are *you,*"
someone asked her pointedly,
and she replied, *I watch.*
"How *is it* for you?" our son
got up his courage and asked you,
hesitant, not wanting to offend.
"I forget this and that," you replied,
"but it doesn't bother me.
I love Margaret, and you, and your sister—
that's what I remember. It's that simple."
Red and gold, the leaves

dance in the air. The tree empties,
the air shines. Love
moves from unmarked box to unmarked box.

MOMENT

Before the adults we call our children arrive with their children in tow
   for Thanksgiving,

we take our morning walk down the lane of oaks and hemlocks, mist,
   a smell of rain by nightfall—underfoot,

the crunch of leathery leaves released by yesterday's big wind.

You're ahead of me, striding into the arch of oaks that opens onto the fields
   and stone walls of the road—

as a V of geese honk a path overhead, and you stop—

in an instant, without thought, raising your arms toward sky, your hands
   flapping from the wrists,

and I can read in the echo your body makes of these wild geese going
   where they must,

such joy, such wordless unity and delight, you are once again the child
   who knows by instinct, by birthright,

just to be is a blessing. In a fictional present, I write the moment down.
   You embodied it.

LUCKY DARK

An uprising . . . a rhapsody of clatter
and renascence, as Stowe's pond, our pond,
pools and seeps
come alive, I say, *with earth music*—pickerels!

I don't know what's wrong,
you say. *I'm confused.*

I've brought you outside for equinox, so we can be like
snakes or spotted
turtles basking in the light,
in love with the angle of the sun and its effects.

Wake up, I tease—it's the vernal orchestra's
Suite for Oboe and Clitoris.

You look across the pond's unshaded clarity,
the bald sun's
bold light, then stare at your hands.

Why is this happening now? You murmur. *I've forgotten.*

And I decide it's time for Whitman's
eloquent attention
to the grass, to the smallest sprout of it.

All goes onward and outward, nothing collapses—
something, something . . .

Out of hopeful green stuff woven, needle by needle
single grass blades—see them?—
prick through
the bleached, matted tangles of winter grass at our feet,

the beautiful uncut hair of graves. . . . . I don't remember
the rest of it.

But surely one can't forget the earth itself, surely we are
bound, if only for a moment's
jubilee,
to all this regeneration and return?

Closeted behind bone, close to the primitive
bark of your brain stem,
there must be a colloquy of cells, pickerel cells,
sweet bells jangled out of tune,
on and off again, shrill. . . .

God of my memory, let me come back as a crocus—open to the sun,
deaf and mute—so that
in the steeply rising light I may sense only scent and gradual
invitation,
nearing sunrise
and bloom without fanfare from my niche in the lucky dark.

Ah, now, here it is—

All goes onward and outward, nothing collapses.
And to die is different from what anyone supposed, and luckier.

A GOOD DEATH

May you
die as did that good man William Blake,

who, shortly before,
broke into singing; before that, called his wife

an angel
and drew not just her face but her whole and spiritual

body. Closer to it,
he said he would forever be near to care for her.

After that, and after the singing, he was still.

Of course, when your good death comes, you'll have
most likely lost

the power of utterance, not a word left to summon,
not a scrap

of whistled melody. No, you will have been for a time
in deepest soliloquy,

in an immense silence, immersed in whatever in us is
powerful, ancient, free.

But since the truth of the imagination for most of us
needs to be

embodied, may you also, while now there's time,
practice dying

before you die. May you daily stand outside time's rush,
whose rivering is

our natural light, and there on the steep lip of what we call
darkness,

call me angel, if angel I am; draw sunbursts in the rainlit air;
sing your heart out.

Great being, radiantly still. And near.

ACKNOWLEDGMENTS

The author expresses gratitude to the editors of the following publications in which the poems listed first appeared: *Blackbird,* "Bed," "Like Ice," "Happiness," "Hard of Hearing," "Remembering," "Summer," "Tasks"; *Georgia Review,* "Sentences," "After," "Revising," and "Solitudes"; *Gettysburg Review,* "Respect"; Hudson Review, "Rosemary"; *Image Journal,* "Broken Cup," "A Good Death"; *Shenandoah,* " Forgetting," "Heaven," "Working with Stone."

I am more grateful than I can say to those whose who out of love and friendship and compassion offered themselves and their time, time and time again, to David and to me as his Alzheimer's progressed. In particular, David's son and daughter, Megan and Josh, for their love and laughter, for their sensitivity and respect, and for their deep loyalty to their father. Thanks to these friends and helpers: Nelson Aldrich, Richard and Phyllis Beauvais, Sidat Balgobin, Jan Beekman, Bob Chapin, Carol Chaput, Dianne Davis, Lynn Gannon, Jacqueline Janes, Ellen Kympton, Gillian Lane-Pleschia, Eleanor Miller, Nancy Neiman-Hoffman, Michael Robertson, Jim and Arlene Scully, and Dr. Rajeesh Tampi.

I wish to thank the early readers of this work: Eamon Grennan, Beverly Jarrett, Rob McQuilken, Ted Deppe, Ted Bent. I have been grateful for many years to all those at Louisiana State University Press who have worked with me, book after book. Thanks especially to John Easterly for his kindness over the years.

NOTES

"Sentences"—"Condemned to accomplish nothing" is from Albert Camus.

"Winter"—Young Rostov and Prince Andrei are characters in Tolstoy's *War and Peace*.

"Far-Hearted"—I came across the word *far-hearted* in an essay by Linda Hogan.

"Respect"—Lines quoted come from books of poems by David McKain: *In Touch* (1975), *The Common Life* (1982), and *Spirit Bodies* (1990).

"House Arrest"—The entire quotation from a letter written by Franz Kafka is this: "You do not even have to leave your room. Remain sitting at your table and listen. Do not even listen, simply wait. Do not even wait, be still and solitary. The world will freely offer itself to you to be unmasked, it has no choice, it will roll in ecstasy at your feet."

"Solitudes"—"Two solitudes that border and protect each other" is from Rilke.

"Simple"—The line from Rumi is given in the translation by Coleman Barks.

"Lucky Dark"—The lines remembered by the speaker come from Walt Whitman's "Song of Myself," section 6.

CPSIA information can be obtained
at www.ICGtesting.com
Printed in the USA
LVHW090619260820
664211LV00015B/1231

9 780807 156421